Soul Secrets

 Kate Brookes

SCHOLASTIC INC.

New York Toronto London Auckland Sydney
Mexico City New Delhi Hong Kong

This edition published in 2000 by
Scholastic Inc. All rights reserved.

A QUARTO CHILDREN'S BOOK
Designed and created by
Quarto Children's Books Ltd
The Fitzpatrick Building,
188-194 York Way, London N7 9QP

Designer: Caroline Grimshaw
Editor: Hazel Songhurst
Art Director:Terry Woodley

ISBN 0-439-22947-2

Printed in China

12 11 10 9 8 7 6 5 4 3 2 1
0 1 2 3 4 5 6 7/0

Contents

All About Soul Secrets

Hi, hello, how are you?

Are you ready to learn about yourself – about your dreams for the future and what kind of friend you are? Do you want to find out what really makes you YOU? With the Soul Secrets kit, and with the help of the Grrrls' Girls, Rella, Roxy, Tutti, and Looie, you and your friends are in for some super soul-revealing fun.

The true you

Discovering what makes you who you are is ultra important. Once you know more about the true you, you will better understand why you act the way you do. And you'll be able to figure out what your dreams are and how to make them come true.

Get ready....

The Soul Secrets kit is packed with things to talk about, think about, and do. As you read the book, check out the items in the kit, and take some time to fill in the Grrrl-to-Grrrl keepsake book. This is where you get to say what you think about all the personal discoveries you've made.

Do the Grrrls' Girl test

As you go through each chapter in Soul Secrets, put it to the Grrrls' Girl test. For example, you should decide if your personality reading really says something about you. You may find that some activities really help you figure out more about the true you, but others are way off. Knowing who you are also means knowing who you're not – keep this in mind!

Are your best buds with you? If not, call them up! This kit is too much fun for one girl, even a go-getter like you!

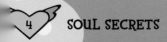

Meet the Grrrls' Girls

Rella, Roxy, Looie, and Tutti are real Grrrls' Girls.
They're going to guide you on your Soul Secrets adventure.

Name: Rella
Best bud: Looie
Favorite saying:
A real princess
believes in love
and fairy tales.

Name: Roxy
Best bud: Tutti
Favorite saying:
You go, girl, you
can be anything
you want to be.

Name: Looie
Best bud: Rella
Favorite saying:
Wild ones follow
their dreams until
they come true.

Name: Tutti
Best bud: Roxy
Favorite saying:
Hello Gorgeous
.... beauty comes
from within.

One of the best things Rella, Roxy, Looie, and Tutti have learned
is that the more they understand their own personalities, the
easier it is to understand their friends. Knowing when a bud
needs lots of hugs, or when it's time for a real serious chat, is
important in making and keeping friendships.

What the symbols mean

Soul Secrets has a ton of cool stuff for you and your best buds to do.
Because there is so much in this kit, the Grrrls' Girls put together a simple
code to make sure you don't miss a thing. Look for these symbols all the
way through the Soul Secrets book.

  When you see the **black-and-white checkered
border** and the green **Action symbol** there is
an **awesome activity** for you to do.

 This symbol marks games that are perfect for **sleepover parties**.

 The **Play It symbol** means that you need to get a special
item out of the kit.

 When you see this symbol, pull out the **Grrrl to Grrrl book**
and get writing!

Getting to Know you

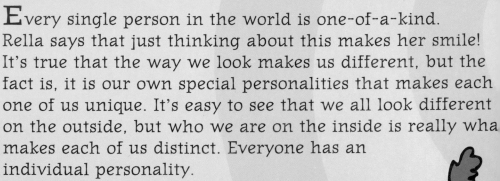

Every single person in the world is one-of-a-kind. Rella says that just thinking about this makes her smile! It's true that the way we look makes us different, but the fact is, it is our own special personalities that makes each one of us unique. It's easy to see that we all look different on the outside, but who we are on the inside is really wha makes each of us distinct. Everyone has an individual personality.

It's EVERYTHING about you

Your personality is what you think, how you behave, and what you do. It's the way you make your buds laugh, or the way you cry at sad movies, and even the way you turn your pizza upside down to eat it! Check out the nine main personality types opposite. When you read them, try to find the one that best matches your personality. This will help you uncover and understand more about the real you!

Pick a profile

Before you look at the personality types, pick three words that describe you, for example, happy, relaxed, sporty. Write them in the Grrrl to Grrrl book. Keep them in mind when you read the type descriptions, and then write down those that come closest to your mini-profile.

It's OK if you find more than one personality that sounds like you. That's part of what makes you who you are!

The nine personality types

Flower girl

You love the peacefulness you find in nature. You hate to see your pals feeling down, and encourage them to talk things through. Conflict upsets you, so you just listen and keep your opinions to yourself.

Peacemaker
You want everything to go perfectly. You hate a messed-up bedroom or a fight with friends. You know how to settle bad vibes between buds, and can spot unfairness a mile off.

Dream doll
You are imaginative and extremely sensitive. You express this in creative arts, and by knowing exactly when a friend needs you. But even dreamers need a reality check.

Sunshine girl
You turn frowns into smiles and make everything sunny-side up! Friends ask for your advice because you're honest and level-headed. But you have to remember that they are there for you, too.

Brain child
You see and question everything, and let your head rule your heart. You think through important decisions. Your friends turn to you for the facts!

Superstar
Onstage you steal the applause; offstage you entertain your buds. You get things done, and fun happens when you're around. You like to keep your cool, but get hotheaded when someone is being dishonest.

The Adventurer
Speed-skating, mountain climbing—you love to test your limits. If you fail on the first try, you get up and try again! The only thing you can't laugh about is boredom, because it is so boring!

Best bud
You put a lot of time into your friendships. Secrets are safe with you, but you also will speak up if a friend is making bad decisions, even if it means saying tough things.

Solo spirit
You won't rest until a problem is solved. Like all true individuals you make your own decisions. Be careful — sometimes you're so independent your buddies can feel left out.

What did the Grrrls' Girls decide?

This is what happened when Looie, Rella, Roxy, and Tutti gave their personalities the once-over!

Looie
I have a great memory, always ask questions, love my buds, adventure, and nature, and I'm a good listener. So I'm a "Brain child," "Adventurer," and "Flower girl."

Rella
It was easy! I would do anything for my friends and I am a bit of a perfectionist. So I guess that makes me a "Best bud" and a "Peacemaker."

Roxy
When it comes to making things happen, I know I am a "Superstar." I can also see myself as one independent "Solo spirit" girl.

Tutti
One side of me is a "Superstar" because I love performing. The other side is "Dream doll" because I'm really sensitive and get swept away by daydreams.

Change can be good

Do you feel different now from the person you were, say, a year ago? It's natural that people change as they grow up, learn more, and experience the world around them. Your personality changes also — sometimes a lot, sometimes just a little. Tutti feels less confident on some days than on others. This doesn't mean that her personality is changing, just that she isn't feeling on top of the world that day. What Tutti does know, though, is that with every new day and new experience, she feels surer about the person she is.

Are you a Grrrls' Girl?

A Grrrls' Girl respects and is honest with herself and always tries to do her best. She is also an honest, loyal, kind, and fun-loving bud who respects her friends. No matter what personality type you are, you can be a Grrrls' Girl.

After you've finished writing your own personality profile on page 3 of your Grrrl to Grrrl book, get your pals to write a profile on you. Compare the profiles to see if they match up. Are you surprised by what your pals wrote? Perhaps you've learned something new and good about yourself as a Grrrls' Girl!

Be true to yourself

When your personality changes from the inside that's natural, but girls know that they are the only ones who can decide who they want to be. Your true friends love and understand you because of the way you are inside. That's why Rella, Tutti, Roxy and Looie are such great girlfriends. They know each other inside out and the qualities that each of them have make each other stronger!

Write it up

Turn to the Grrrl to Grrrl book and write down what you think about your personality choices. In a few months, look back at what you wrote. Does it still hold true? If not, read over the nine personality types again to find the changing you.

Dream Grrrls

Roxy, Rella, Tutti and Looie, are always telling each other their dream stories. Dreams are so amazing! The coolest part is trying to figure out what they might mean. So, the girls decided to decode their dreams. They did some research and found out a lot about what dreams might mean and how they can help you to understand what's on your mind. Now, they're going to share everything they learned with you.

Dream mail

Having a dream is like getting a special message from you, to you! There are all kinds of messages you can get from a dream. Some help you to understand how you feel about something, or help you to make a big decision, others replay important things that happened to you, or reveal your deepest desires.

Dream on, gorgeous!
Hey, girls! Wake up and sneak-a-peek at
some of these fabulous dream facts!

 You and your buds spend a third of your life sleeping.

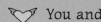 Everyone dreams – even tiny babies before they are born.
The tricky part is remembering your dreams; not
everyone can.

 Dreaming is really good for you, even if you do not
remember the dream. It lets your mind work through all
the events of the day.

 Dream experts believe that really good friends can
dream the same dream at the same time.

Dream patterns

Write down your dreams for a couple of
weeks (or even longer), then see if you can
find a pattern. Do some images come up again and
again? Some dreams are like the episodes in a TV soap:
Each one ends with a cliffhanger, and you won't
know the happy ending until you've seen every
episode! Sometimes you'll have the same dream over
and over like the rerun of an old movie. This often
means something really big is on your mind!

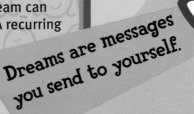

The people who study dreams divide them
into different types. For example, a creative
dream is filled with pictures that can inspire
a story or painting. A predictive dream can
show the dreamer a future event. A recurring
dream is one that you have over
and over again.

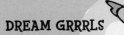
Dreams are messages
you send to yourself.

Dream symbols

Look for the symbols that match closest with your dream. Read the meanings, then link them together to try and understand your dream.

Symbols

Cake—this means something yummy is coming your way.

Fireworks—this symbolizes the goals you've set and know you can achieve.

Galloping horse—this means you need freedom or time alone.

Notebook—you need to write down a great idea.

People

Artist—this means use your talent and creativity.

Baby—this means something new is coming into your life.

Family—you might be thinking about someone close.

Smiling friends—this says that your buds are a great team.

Action

Combing hair—you are searching for a solution.

Flying—this symbolizes that you are feeling confident.

Running straight — this shows that you know what you want.

Stroking a pet—this means someone close needs you.

Places

Beach—this tells you that fun is coming, but also to be careful.

Crossroads— this shows you have a decision to make.

Kitchen— this shows how important your family is to you.

Small room—this shows that you may be trying to understand something about yourself.

Emotions

Anger—this symbolizes something that is upsetting you and needs dealing with, fast!

Feeling confident—this shows you are looking good and feeling just great about yourself.

Being hugged—this symbolizes love and friendships and being open about your feelings.

Happiness—this shows that any problems you have might get worse but then disappear.

It's a sleepover

When you and your buddies get together for a sleepover, compare your dreams as soon as you all wake up. (This, of course, means that you have to get some sleep!) It'll be a ton of fun, and you never know what you might discover about each other! Maybe your friends will be able to interpret your favorite dream!

Try this

Have you ever thought how great it would be to control your dreams, or at least make sure they're always going to be awesome? Then try this: Before you fall asleep, close your eyes and imagine yourself performing a truly great stunt! It could be mastering your back flip on the trampoline, or even making a cake for your mom's birthday! Whatever it is has to be upbeat, positive, and real—and it will help your dreams to be just as inspiring.

Make your dreams come true!

Dream diary

Use the dream diary sheets in the kit to write down your dreams. Use the dream symbols in the Pillow Talk section to help you interpret them. This is a cool way to get to grips with anything that's bugging you. It's also great for keeping track of all the fantastic ideas your mind creates when you're asleep!

Listen up!

Not everything in a dream has a hidden meaning. Most dreams are connected to events that happen in your everyday life.

By the numbers

Listen up! You're going to find out something really cool about numbers. But don't worry, this is not homework! Would you believe that numbers have a power all their own? They can give you cool insider info about a lot of things, including the kind of friend you are. Read on to connect with your key number and its meaning.

Connecting with your key number

Finding your key number is sooo simple! If Tutti can do it, so can you! Here's how it works:

Step 1
Write your name on a piece of paper. Then match each letter to the correct number using the Letter-Number Code on the next page. Mark the numbers under the letters of your name.

23229

Step 2
Add up the numbers. Tutti's name adds up to 18. If your name adds up to a single digit, then that's your key number.

23229 = 18

Step 3
If your name adds up to a two-digit number (10 or more), add the digits of your number together. Tutti's number was 18, so she added 1+8. Her key number is 9. If your number is still 10 or more, keep adding the digits together until you get one single number.

?

Step 4
Check out your key number in Cracking the code to see what sort of bud you are.

Letter-number code

A	1	J	1	S	1
B	2	K	2	T	2
C	3	L	3	U	3
D	4	M	4	V	4
E	5	N	5	W	5
F	6	O	6	X	6
G	7	P	7	Y	7
H	8	Q	8	Z	8
I	9	R	9		

YOU can be anything you want to be

racking the code

our key number tells you what kind of friend you are, but it also ɛveals your hot dates — days in the month when amazing things will appen to you! Plus, you'll learn your coolest day of the week. You will lso find out the key numbers that are your top friendship matches.

1 Super storyteller Your buds love your stories. You can turn a awn-fest into a laugh-riot, and you always leave them laughing. ou are super-social and would rather be hanging out with friends han on your own. You're generous with everything and have smiles or everyone.
ot dates: 1st, 10th, 19th. Coolest day: Sunday. Top friendship numbers: 1, 2, 9.

2 Loyal listener What a true friend you are! You're the perfect ud because when you listen, you totally understand. You're caring and ɔyal, and are willing to trust your buds with your deepest secrets. ven if you aren't a girl's best friend, she might choose you to confide ı. She knows you'll understand.
ot dates: 2nd, 20th, 29th. Coolest day: Monday. Top friendship numbers: 2, 4, 8.

3 Affectionate friend You're a supersweet bud who greets her als with huge hugs every time you see them. You always make your ˙iends feel special by sharing your time and anything else they might eed. But you rarely ask them for help when you need it. No need to ʻorry — they'll be there for you, too.
ot dates: 3rd, 21st, 30th. Coolest day: Thursday. Top friendship numbers: 7, 8,

✿4 Problem-solving pal

You have a talent for seeing a situation from all sides. This makes you a great problem-solver, and your friends rely on you to share your thoughtful advice. Occasionally, a friend might be shocked by your honesty, but you'll always stand up for what you think is right.

Hot dates: 4th, 22nd, 31st. Coolest day: Sunday.
Top friendship numbers: 2, 4, 7.

✿5 Fun friend

You're super-supportive. You encourage your friends and cheer them on in whatever they do. You love hanging out, and you usually organize every girlie get-together. Your belief is, the more friends, the more fun.

Hot dates: 5th, 14th, 23rd. Coolest day: Wednesday.
Top friendship numbers: 5, 6, 9.

✿6 Angel with attitude

You're a devoted bud who'd do anything for her friends, but you also have a feisty fearless streak. Even though you're supersweet, you love your independence and never mind doing things on your own.

Hot dates: 6, 18, 27. Coolest day: Friday. Top friendship numbers: 1, 3, 6.

✿7 One-of-a-kind open mind

Your buds love your upbeat attitude. You're easygoing and don't usually seek out new friends on your own. Most of the time, a new friend will decide to become your bud. Girls like to hang with you because you have interesting ideas and an open mind.

Hot dates: 7th, 16th, 25th.
Coolest day: Monday.
Top friendship numbers: 3, 4, 7.

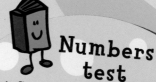

Numbers test

First, figure out if your friends' key numbers match your friendship numbers. Then sticker your hot dates and coolest days on a calendar. Keep the calendar up-to-date with what's going on in your life and check to see if your hot dates and coolest days were better than the rest! Use pages 4 and 5 of the Grrrl to Grrrl book to record how close the numbers matched your coolest days, hottest dates, and best buddies!

✽ 8 True blue

You're loyal to your buds and couldn't imagine a day without talking to them. You know that true friendships don't just happen, they need time, honesty, and trust. Once you make a friend, you're true blue. Even when a bud moves away you let her know you'll always be there for her.

Hot dates: 8th, 17th, 26th. Coolest day: Saturday.

Top friendship numbers: 1, 5, 8.

Numbers on the run

To entertain your buds when you're out and about and traveling light, play the numbers game using the five cards in the kit. Don't forget to pack a pad and pencil— it'll make figuring out the key numbers a breeze.

✿ 9 Bodacious bud

You are one very cool buddy, full of fun and funky ideas. You've always got new plans for your friends, and they love your sense of adventure. If a bud's feeling blue, you'll think of something fun to cheer her up.

Hot dates: 9th, 18th, 30th. Coolest day: Tuesday. Top friendship numbers: 3, 6, 9.

Do the numbers add up?

You know already that Tutti's key number is 9. But what about Roxy, Looie, and Rella? So, is it true that Roxy is a fun 1, Looie a true 2, Rella a chatty 3, and Tutti a fine 9? Can playing the numbers game really tell you more about your personality, hot dates, and best buds?

Destiny Dealer

Get some friends together and grab the Destiny Dealer from the kit.

1. Ask a friend to pick a color. Then open and close the Dealer as you spell out the letters in the color.
2. Next, your bud picks a number, and you open and close the Dealer that number of times.
3. Now ask your bud to choose another number. You lift up the flap to reveal their destiny!

Yours truly

If you're like Roxy, Rella, Tutti, and Looie, there are times when you know exactly where you're heading and why. Then, there are moments when you feel as if you are being pulled in two directions at once, or doing something that seems way out of character. Why? Well, maybe Chinese astrology holds some of the answers! It says that everyone has an inner and an outer personality — two personalities that can be completely different from one another.

Two sides of your personality

Because the inner and outer you can be very different, sometimes the things you do can conflict with your deepest feelings. For example, on the outside, Tutti is an extrovert who seems superconfident when she's performing in a play. But inside, Tutti is not always so sure of herself, and she's surprised that she feels so relaxed in front of an audience. But when Tutti checked out her Chinese astrology, she found that the animal signs for her inner and outer personalities were very different indeed!

Roxy found her two animal signs were identical — meaning that her inner and outer personalities are exactly the same! This makes sense, because Roxy is one girl who is totally comfortable with everything she does.

Chinese astrology

Chinese astrology is linked to twelve different animals. The animals connect to the hour, month, and year in which you were born. The Chinese believe that the time you were born says something about your outer personality. The month and year in which you were born determine the inner you. This is considered your true personality.

How to find your readings

You can discover your outer personality by finding the hour of your birth on the Hour Chart. Then, move on to the Month and Year Chart. This chart will connect your birth date to the animal sign that represents your inner personality. There's a lot to remember, so be sure to write down the animals for both your inner and your outer personalities. Next, turn to the Outer and Inner You section on the next page.

Hour Chart

sk a parent to tell you what me of the day or night you ere born. Then, ask if you ere born during Daylight aving Time. If you were, you hould move your time f birth back one hour when ou are finding your animal. ach animal sign relates to a ifferent two-hour period.

Hour of birth	Animal
1 pm to 12:59 am	Rat
am to 2:59 am	Ox
am to 4:59 am	Tiger
am to 6:59 am	Rabbit
am to 8:59 am	Dragon
am to 10:59 am	Snake
1 am to 12:59 pm	Horse
pm to 2:59 pm	Sheep
pm to 4:59 pm	Monkey
pm to 6:59 pm	Rooster
pm to 8:59 pm	Dog
pm to 10:59 pm	Pig

Month and Year Chart

Month and year of birthday	Animal
February 13, 1983—February 1, 1984	Pig
February 2, 1984—February 19, 1985	Rat
February 20, 1985—February 8, 1986	Ox
February 9, 1986—January 28, 1987	Tiger
January 29, 1987—February 16, 1988	Rabbit
February 17, 1988—February 5, 1989	Dragon
February 6, 1989—January 26, 1990	Snake
January 27, 1990—February 14, 1991	Horse
February 15, 1991—February 3, 1992	Sheep
February 4, 1992—January 22, 1993	Monkey
January 23, 1993—February 9, 1994	Rooster
February 10, 1994—January 30, 1995	Dog
January 31, 1995—February 18, 1996	Pig
February 19, 1996—February 7, 1997	Rat
February 8, 1997—January 27, 1998	Ox
January 28, 1998—February 15, 1999	Tiger
February 16, 1999—February 4, 2000	Rabbit
February 5, 2000—January 23, 2001	Dragon
January 24, 2001—February 11, 2002	Snake

The Outer and Inner You

Remember, you get the inner you from the year you were born and the outer you from the time of your birth. Got it? Cool! Now check out their meanings below.

Rat
You like to talk about anything that is bothering you and encourage your friends to do the same. This is because you want them to be as happy and carefree as you are.

Ox
You're a true eco-girl. You are caring and gentle with any creature or plant, but you can be forceful with those who don't respect nature.

Tiger
You're a go-getter, constantly closing in on your goals. But be careful—being so focused means you sometimes miss out on being part of a team!

Rabbit
You're way creative and expressive, and you've got this knack for creating enthusiasm for an idea, so everyone wants to get involved.

Dragon
You hate being unprepared, late, or rushed—it makes you stressed. But being organized means that you are always ready for fun and lots of it!

Snake
You are more comfortable letting others be the center of attention. You're not quiet or shy— you're introspective and listen to your inner voice instead of others.

Horse
You're a free spirit who doesn't want to be tied down. Your love of adventure and of meeting different people makes you open-minded.

Sheep
You aim high and your dreams are ambitious. You want to do things just right and never settle for anything less than perfect.

Monkey
Truthfulness is ultra important to you. You are willing to share the truth with friends, even if it hurts, because you believe honesty is the basis of real friendship.

Rooster
You are into whatever is popular now, and you don't care what other people say about the fads. You may love attention, but you are also intelligent, honest, and straightforward.

Dog
You are compassionate, loyal, and a good listener who would never let down a friend. You are the first to speak up against injustice.

Pig
You are a true believer who always thinks the best of your buds. You are open, caring, and giving, and would do anything for a friend.

What do you think?

Does Chinese astrology hold the answer? If your outer and inner personalities are wildly different, does it explain why you sometimes have trouble making a decision or knowing what to do? Would you like to be more like your inner or your outer personality? Or, do you like the way you are — a combination of both?

Animal match

Record your and your best bud's animal signs in the Grrrl to Grrrl book. Think about the descriptions of your inner and outer personalities, and write about whether they were a perfect match or a total miss!

What Rella and Looie think

Should you let your true self hide behind your public personality? Looie thinks that if you are more comfortable with one side of your personality, then it's okay if you decide to let that side shine more. Maybe it's that you like to keep all your deepest and fondest dreams as part of your inner personality. Rella doesn't believe anyone should try to hide anything, especially their dreams. She likes to know as much as she can about her friends so she can be a better bud, but she also knows that everyone is different.

YOU know yourself!

You make it happen

Don't accept what you read here word for word! Your knowledge of yourself and what you want is much more powerful than any prediction of your personality.

YOURS TRULY

Write on, Grrrl!

Did you know that it's not just what you write that expresses your thoughts, but it's also how you write it? Whether your handwriting is large or small, ultra-neat (like Rella's), or a total mess (like Looie's!), your handwriting is unique. It reveals all kinds of things — from the kind of person you are, to your likes and dislikes and even your mood!

Read on!

A person's handwriting style is full of clues about her personality. Here are some styles and some of the things they say.

Try this

Grab your girls and see if you can imitate each other's writing. It sounds easy until you look really close at a friend's script and notice how she dots her i's, crosses her t's, and how her writing slants in a totally different direction from yours. You may know what your bud's writing looks like, but it's hard to imitate because everyone's writing style is different. It's something that develops naturally.

Best Bud

- •Very large writing: You are outgoing and generous, but if you are not careful you can be bossy.
- •Very small writing: You are patient and shy. You are more comfortable expressing yourself in writing than in speech.
- •Writing slants right: You are a good communicator.
- •Writing is upright: You are stable and independent.
- •Writing slants left: You are thoughtful and shy.
- •Square, even letters: You are good with numbers.
- •Rounded with loops: You are creative and artistic.
- •I's dotted with circles: You are into details.

Mixed messages

When you write, your brain sends out messages to the muscles in your hand. Some are about what you want to write; others are messages about how you're feeling. If you're stressed and angry, your brain reacts in such a way that it alters your handwriting. For example, the muscles in your hand will tense up and you'll hold the pen tightly and press really hard. When you're relaxed, and happy, your muscles are relaxed too, and your writing will look totally different.

Love or hate

Write about something you like a lot — a new outfit, your favorite song or TV show. Then write about something that bugs you — such as having tons of homework, or when your sister borrows your clothes! Now, look at both pieces. Can you see the differences? The letters in your stressed writing are probably jagged and closer together. On the other hand, your happy writing shows that you're relaxed, because the letters are more rounded and the spacing more even.

Oodles of doodles

Most people doodle when they talk on the phone or are figuring out a problem. Could your doodles have special meaning? Look through this list to find out.

• *Butterflies* Freedom and independence are important to you.
• *Coloring in circles and loops* You like to finish whatever you start.
• *Flowers* Everything is total bliss.
• *Boxes around words* You're organized and practical.

• *Arrows* You're busy and you know there are things you just gotta do.
• *Hearts* You're thinking about someone special.
• *Underlining* Your creativity is showing, but what you underline indicates your true interests.

Get writing!

So, are you ready to do the quiz and check out what your handwriting says about your mood? All you need is a sample of your normal writing style. When the Grrrls' Girls did this, they each wrote a page about their bedrooms — what they really liked and what they would like to change. But you and your friends might want to write about something else. Use unlined paper and a ballpoint or roller-ball pen.

Come on, express yourself!

What's your mood?

This quiz hints at how you were feeling at the exact moment you did the writing and how that can affect your long-term take on life. Answer the six questions by choosing A, B, or C.

Is your handwriting ...
○ **A** fast forward — does it slant to the right?
○ **B** straight up and down?
○ **C** laid back — does it slant to the left?

Does your writing ...
○ **A** move up the page?
○ **B** go straight across?
○ **C** slide down the page?

Are the i's dotted ...
○ **A** high?
○ **B** in just about the right place?
○ **C** really low?

Are the t's crossed ...
○ **A** high?
○ **B** in the middle?
○ **C** low?

Is the bar crossing the t ...
○ **A** pointing up?
○ **B** straight?
○ **C** pointing down?

Is your writing ...
○ **A** large?
○ **B** medium?
○ **C** small?

Do you decorate your writing?
○ **A** Always?
○ **B** Sometimes?
○ **C** Never?

be the girl you wanna be™

SOUL SECRETS

Quiz answers

❄ **Mostly As** When you wrote this, your confidence level was way up, and your ambitions were sky-high! Maybe you were looking forward to something, or maybe you had just reached a goal you were really proud of. If your writing generally looks like this, you are a real go-getter. The down side is that you often take on too much and stress yourself out trying to accomplish it all. Be kind to yourself by tackling your goals one at a time.

✿ **Mostly Bs** There's a pretty good chance you were just cruisin' through life when you wrote your page. Nothing was bugging you, and you were feeling ultra calm about what's going on in your world. If your writing usually looks like this, you are someone who sets realistic goals and you know you can meet them without working up a sweat. You're not into making snap decisions. You weigh everything, making sure you know the whole story before doing anything. This is why your pals see you as the "sensible one."

✿ **Mostly Cs** You were probably feeling laid back when you wrote your page. If your writing looks like this most of the time, you are a cool, relaxed type of girl. You don't let things get to you. You might even forget about some things that upset you because you don't want to make a big deal about it. You have mega dreams, but you are content to slowly work toward them. Instead of sharing all your big ideas with your friends, you often keep them to yourself.

Sign up

Keep a check on your handwriting (and your best buddies') by having everyone sign her autograph in the Grrrl to Grrrl book (pages 6 to 9). Don't forget to date them and, in a couple of years, you can all look back and compare your current signatures to the earlier ones. Each one of you should include a special message, too.

You know, as you grow and your personality develops, your writing goes through changes, too!

WRITE ON, GRRRL!

25

Body talk

Have you ever noticed how much you can learn about people just by watching them? For example, it's easy to tell when your best bud has had a really good day — her shoulders are back, her chin is up, and a smile lights up her fabulous face. But did you know that keeping an eye out for body language can also help you to uncover a person's inner personality and deepest thoughts? So, do you want to know more? Then listen up!

Every body movement tells a secret

It's amazing to think about, but your mind can transmit secret messages through your body! The way a person sits, stands, or folds her arms communicates things that she might never say out loud. If you learn how to read a person's body language, you'll have a better idea what that person is really, truly thinking. Take a look at the 2 Grrrls Dictionary of Body Language and see.

Try this

1 Look in a mirror. Picture a plain, white wall. Relax your face so you have a blank expression.

2 Imagine you are at a party! Your favorite music is playing, and you're feeling excited....

3 Now look in the mirror! Your hidden, happy thoughts have appeared all over your face!

Buddy talk

Pick a day for you and a friend to log each other's body moves. Draw stick figures to show poses and facial expressions, and write down how you think your bud is feeling. Stick the drawings into the Grrrl to Grrrl book and fill in what your body language expressed.

The 2 Grrrls Dictionary of Body Language

See if you can guess the body language of a girl who is:
*paying attention *happy *stressed out *nervous
*totally annoyed! *won't listen *really likes you

Expression
- Wide-open grin: *very happy*
- Big smile: *pleased, welcoming*
- Unsmiling, biting lip: *nervous, shy, stressed*
- Mouth turned down: *unhappy, angry, stubborn*
- Tight-closed mouth: *very angry*
- Gentle smile: *relaxed, trusting*
- Tight-pursed lips: *very stressed*

Eyes
- Wide open: *happy, excited*
- Gazing into yours: *welcoming, trusting*
- Looking down: *nervous, unsure*
- Staring away: *very angry, very stressed*
- Looking away: *thinking, daydreaming, defensive*
- Wide open, making eye contact: *alert, attentive*
- Avoiding eye contact: *angry, shy*

Legs and feet
- Feet together: *alert, tense, attentive*
- Legs and feet apart: *happy, relaxed*
- Legs and feet slightly apart: *welcoming, shy, trusting*
- Ankles crossed tightly: *stressed, nervous, defensive*
- Legs crossed tightly at the knee: *tense, shy*
- Legs or ankles crossed lightly: *relaxed, calm*

Arms and hands
- Arms raised, palms open: *happy, excited*
- Arms folded: *shy, nervous*
- Arms folded tightly, hands hidden: *defensive, unhappy, angry, stressed*
- Hands clasped tightly: *very angry, stressed*
- Hands folded gently: *relaxed, alert*
- Arms open, palms upturned: *trusting, open*

Posture
- Shoulders relaxed: *happy, calm*
- Head tilted: *welcoming, listening*
- Head lowered: *nervous, unhappy*
- Head turned, tilted up: *not listening, daydreaming*
- Shoulders up or slouched forward: *angry, stressed, defensive*
- Leaning forward: *alert, attentive*
- Rubbing neck: *nervous, stressed*

Body alert!

Knowing how to read and use body language can be useful, as the Grrrls' Girls found out.

Sign reading

Rella needed an extension on her report but could tell her teacher was totally stressed—his shoulders were rounded and he was rubbing his neck. If she asked him then, he would say no! So, she waited until he was more relaxed, and he said yes!

Looking deeper

When a new family moved in next door, the girl acted real tough, but Looie noticed how she was biting her lip, folding her arms, and crossing her ankles. Looie realized she was just nervous about being "the new girl", so she made her feel welcome, and now they're good friends.

Feeling good

Roxy's mom was feeling nervous about a job interview. Roxy told her that if she looked confident she would feel confident. When her mom held her head high and put on a big smile, Roxy knew she would get the job!

Bad act

Tutti was in the school play but couldn't get her "bad-girl" act right. When the drama coach suggested she stand around with her arms tightly crossed, shoulders up, and her head turned away, Tutti's character came to life!

Photo call

Check out some group photos from your scrapbook and discover the truth! Was your smiling bud really dying of embarrassment in that turkey outfit at the costume party? Was anyone actually listening to the coach before the basketball game? And who has a secret crush?

Change your mood!

Actors exaggerate their body language to help their performance and to help them feel more like the character they are playing. You can see if this works for you — how do you feel when you strike an angry pose? Or a happy pose? Do different poses make you *feel* different?

Do you believe that if you look happy you'll feel happy? Next time you're feeling down, turn on a smile and you might just turn your mood around! Plus, smiles are infectious: If you smile at someone, they'll smile back! The not-so-hot news is that bad moods can be infectious, too! Next time your bud is having a bad day, don't let her mood get you, too! Instead, give her a big, big smile and a warm, loving hug. Then stand back and watch her bad mood disappear!

Try this

Choose one girl to be the first "actor." When everyone shouts "Action!" she must act out an emotion using body language. SHE IS NOT ALLOWED TO MAKE ANY KIND OF SOUND! The audience must read her body language and work out the emotion! The girl who guesses right then gets her chance to be the star.

What A Friend

Feel good!

If you're having a bad day, use the "Girls Feel Good" stickers in the kit to give yourself (or your bud) an ego boost! Stick them on your mirror, school bag, or the back of your hand! Each time you see a **2 GRRRLS** sticker, a smile will cross your fabulous face!

Girl Power

be the girl you wanna be

Stand up and be noticed!

Every picture tells a story

Have you and a bud ever looked at a picture and seen it in a totally different way? Maybe you saw a beautiful snowflake, but your friend spotted a bunch of daisies! Just because you saw different things doesn't mean one of you was right or wrong. It's just that you both interpreted the picture in your own unique way!

What's on your mind?

Because every person sees things differently, the images that you do see can say a lot about the inner you.
An easy way to find out if you think this theory is true is by using inkblot pictures. If you don't know what inkblot pictures are, read on....

Cool patterns

An inkblot picture isn't a picture of anything real, it's just a blob of ink that creates a cool pattern. When you look at an inkblot it will quickly remind you of something. The first image that pops into your head says something about you – about your personality, your mood, or even about what is currently on your mind.

Spot the blot

Scientists believe that the images people see in inkblots can say something about the kind of person they are:

* **The big picture** — Girls who are clever and inventive often see whole images of people.
* **Color perfect** — Girls with an artistic eye will often see colors first and shapes second.
* **It's a small world** — Thoughtful girls may see lots of tiny images instead of one larger picture.
* **On the move** — Girls who are imaginative see images that feature a lot of movement.

How to make an inkblot

Ask an adult to help you with this! You will need the sheet of inkblot paper and inkblot folder in the kit, newspaper, black and colored ink, scissors, a pen and a small spoon. If you prefer, you can use watered-down paint instead of ink.

Step 1
Lay a sheet of newspaper under the inkblot paper. Using a spoon, drop blobs or wiggly lines of ink or paint into the center of your inkblot paper. (An X marks the center.) You can use one, two, or even three colors of ink or paint.

Step 2
Fold the paper in half and press it gently (this will spread the paint across the page). Then, unfold the paper and leave the inkblot to dry. Do not look at it!

Step 3
Cut along the dotted lines on the inkblot folder to form four flaps, and slide the dry inkblot inside.

Step 4
Pass the folder between you and your pals. Under each flap, write down the image that jumps into your head when you see the inkblot. Close the flap, and pass on the folder. Then open all the flaps to read what everyone saw.

Test it out!

Can you figure out the meaning behind your inkblot reading? Does it relate to something that has happened to you? Do you know why your friends saw what they did? Keep in mind that there are no right or wrong answers — every answer is the right one for that person.

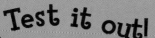

Try this
Once you know what your pals saw in the inkblots, try to see if you can spot their inkblot images, too!

You're a star

Every girl feels superspecial on her birthday. But did you know that your birthday can actually say something about the kind of person you are? Some people believe that the position of the sun, moon, and planets on the day you were born can reveal details about your personality. You've probably heard about the zodiac. Want to put it to the Grrrls' Girls test? Then grab your buds and read on....

Are you starstruck?

You make it happen!

The ancient study of the stars and how they affect us and our lives is called astrology. Astrology is based on the twelve constellations that make up the signs of the zodiac. (A constellation is a group of stars that are named after the shapes they make in the sky.) Astrologers believe that the sign you were born under gives you certain personality traits and affects your destiny, too.

You're a star every day!

What do you think? Is your personality influenced by your birthday? Could the position of the stars on the day you were born influence everything from your unique talents to your taste in clothes?

I think I'm a natural performer.

Wait up, I'll see if that matches your star sign.

It's written in the stars!

Looie, Rella, Roxy, and Tutti always read the horoscopes in their fave magazines. They like to check out what is supposed to happen in their lives. Sometimes their horoscopes are right on target, and sometimes they are way wrong! And here's why: For a horoscope to show the true influence of the stars, an astrologer must work out the exact position of the sun, moon, and planets at the very moment someone was born. This means that everyone has a totally unique horoscope!

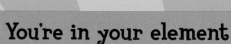

Girls are stargazing!

You're in your element

In addition to the twelve zodiac signs, there are four elements that contribute to your unique horoscope: air, earth, fire, and water. These are the vital building blocks of our planet — we couldn't exist without them! Each element has a special meaning and is linked to a star sign. When you've read through the Starstruck chart on the next two pages, find the element logo that matches your star sign, then come back here to check out what it says about you.

Air	Earth	Fire	Water

You are a smart and logical thinker, yet you are still idealistic. You set goals that are sky-high.	You are a dependable and trustworthy person, practical and intelligent. And, most of all, you are down-to-earth.	You are creative and enthusiastic, and your love of life sends out rays of happiness — just like the sun!	You are a sensitive and caring person. Your friends know your generosity is as constant as the rivers flowing to the sea.

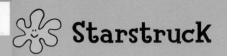 # Starstruck

Look for the sign that includes your birthday, and read what it says about you. Then read the other signs and decide if your star reading is really the best match for you.

Star rating: You'll climb every mountain — and reach the top!
CAPRICORN (Earth)
December 22 to January 20
• Symbol: The Goat
• Key traits: Hardworking, determined, and levelheaded.
• Secret wish: To be everything you want to be!

Star rating: You're super-caring and one of a kind!
AQUARIUS (Air)
January 21 to February 18
• Symbol: The Water Carrier
• Key traits: Friendly, intelligent, and a real livewire.
• Secret wish: That everyone would want world peace.

Star rating: You can get lost in your own active imagination!
PISCES (Water)
February 19 to March 20
• Symbol: Two Fishes
• Key traits: Sympathetic, popular, and a perfectionist.
• Secret wish: To love math and science as much as music and art.

Star rating: Your head is filled with great ideas!
ARIES (Fire)
March 21 to April 20
• Symbol: The Ram
• Key traits: Inventive, energetic, and totally truthful.
• Secret wish: To always have a unique view of the world.

Star rating: You're happiest in the great outdoors!
TAURUS (Earth)
April 21 to May 21
• Symbol: The Bull
• Key traits: Loyal, sensible, and generous.
• Secret wish: A safe habitat for all wildlife.

Star rating: You're always ready for life's surprises.
GEMINI (Air)
May 22 to June 21
• Symbol: The Twins
• Key traits: Energetic, creative, and reliable.
• Secret wish: To learn about everything and anything!

If you're a girl who was born in the first or last days of a zodiac sign, you're probably a cosmic mixture of the two signs you are closest to!

Star rating: You're a girl whose friends mean everything!
CANCER (Water)
June 22 to July 22
• Symbol: The Crab
• Key traits: Sympathetic, artistic, and thoughtful.
• Secret wish: To really help the people you care about.

Star rating: You're searching for a sunny, perfect world.
LEO (Fire)
July 23 to August 23
• Symbol: The Lion
• Key traits: Outgoing, confident, and clever.
• Secret wish: That everyone could realize how special they are.

Star rating: You're a sporty girl who loves a challenge.
VIRGO (Earth)
August 24 to September 22
• Symbol: The Maiden
• Key traits: Honest, quick-witted, ambitious.
• Secret wish: To play your best for the love of the game.

Star rating: You believe in the power of peace and harmony.
LIBRA (Air)
September 23 to October 23
• Symbol: The Scales
• Key traits: Mellow, sensitive, and kind.
• Secret wish: To keep your best buds forever.

Star rating: You're a girl who is true to herself.
SCORPIO (Water)
October 24 to November 22
• Symbol: The Scorpion
• Key traits: Dynamic, inspiring, and warm-hearted.
• Secret wish: To understand more about people and the world.

Star rating: You have the travel bug and love new experiences.
SAGITTARIUS (Fire)
November 23 to December 21
• Symbol: The Archer
• Key traits: Optimistic, inventive, and sincere.
• Secret wish: To make everyone laugh!

True friendships are made in the heart, not in the stars.

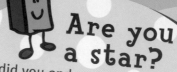

Are you a star?

Shooting stars

Your zodiac sign also has a big influence on your friendships and true love! When two people are really right for one another, people say their relationship is "a match made in heaven." This phrase means that their star signs are totally in tune with each other. Look down the chart to see who might be your star-match best buds, and who could be your love for life!

Star Buds Chart

Star Sign	Best Buds	Completely Crushworthy
Capricorn	Taurus, Aries	Virgo
Aquarius	Gemini, Libra	Aquarius
Pisces	Aries, Scorpio	Cancer
Aries	Libra, Sagittarius	Leo
Taurus	Capricorn, Virgo	Taurus
Gemini	Gemini, Sagittarius	Libra
Cancer	Scorpio, Cancer	Pisces
Leo	Aquarius, Leo	Sagittarius
Virgo	Pisces, Taurus	Capricorn
Libra	Aquarius, Aries	Gemini
Scorpio	Cancer, Pisces	Aries
Sagittarius	Leo, Aquarius	Sagittarius

We'll be best friends forever!

Elements attract

Don't be surprised if your buds are the same element as you. Buds who have the same element sign usually get along great together. Other good matchups are Air and Fire, and Earth and Water.

Match it up

You can use the Star Buds Chart to figure out who your ideal buds are according to the zodiac matches. You can also find the sign of your most compatible crush. Turn to pages 12 and 13 of the Grrrl to Grrrl book and write down their star signs. Do the signs for your ideal friends and most compatible crush match those of your real best buds and current crush?

Spin the Star Wheel

In the kit, you'll find the Star Wheel. Grab hold of it and keep it with you at all times. You can use it to check out your star-buddy-crush readings anytime, anyplace! It's a cinch to use – just spin the disk until the colors and the symbols line up.

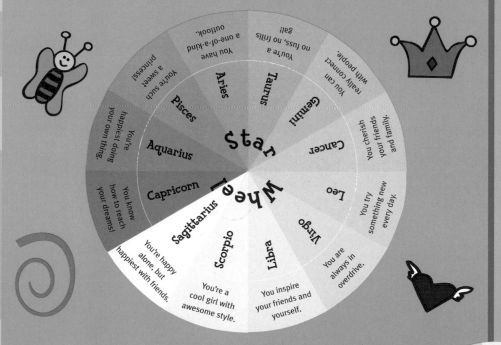

Aries — You're such a sweet princess!
Taurus — You have a one-of-a-kind outlook.
Gemini — You're a no fuss, no frills gal!
Cancer — You can really connect with people.
Leo — You cherish your friends and family.
Virgo — You try something new every day.
Libra — You are always in overdrive.
Scorpio — You inspire your friends and yourself.
Sagittarius — You're a cool girl with awesome style.
Capricorn — You're happy alone, but happiest with friends.
Aquarius — You know how to reach your dreams!
Pisces — You're happiest doing your own thing.

Star Wheel

Tea-leaf time

Reading tea leaves is an ancient way of predicting the future. All you do is drink a cup of tea and ask a question. The tea leaves will form a pattern in the cup, and you can figure out the answer to your question by interpreting what the pattern means.

Did I ace the math test?

Will my team win their game?

Remember this!
The tea leaves can only predict things happening 24 hours into the future.

The tea party

※ **Step 1** Ask an adult to help you make a pot of tea using loose-leaf tea (tea bags won't work). Pour a cup for everyone, but don't strain out the leaves. They need to stay in the cup, so you can read the pattern they make when you are done. It's best to use small teacups.

※ **Step 2** When it's cool enough, drink your tea. You should leave just enough liquid in the bottom of the cup to cover the leaves. To make the fortune your very own, you have to drink the tea yourself.

※ **Step 3** Hold the cup in your left hand. Think about your question and swirl the cup three times counterclockwise. You don't have to keep your question secret. Your buds can help you spot the tea-leaf pictures.

Does my crush like me?

※ **Step 4** Turn the cup upside down onto a saucer and let the liquid drain. It's OK if some of the leaves drop into the saucer. Turn the cup back up again, and you're all ready to start your reading.

Will my Gramma Nellie visit?

What the leaves say

The tea leaves don't give simple "yes" or "no" answers. Instead, each picture has a meaning. To work out the answer to your question, turn the cup this way and that to see the picture-shapes, then look at the meanings.

☆ **Arch:** You and your buddies are in this together.

☆ **Bird:** You are going to hear some wickedly wonderful news.

☆ **Boat:** Roll out the welcome mat for a visitor from far away.

☆ **Circle:** A surprise package has YOUR name on it.

☆ **Crescent moon:** Someone is totally wowed by your charms.

☆ **Square:** You should take a break and let yourself relax in some peaceful vibes.

☆ **Tree:** Something you wished for has happened.

☆ **Triangle:** Your hard work will lead to success. You go, girl!

☆ **Heart:** There's a new crush in your life.

☆ **Three-leaf clover:** Good fortune is coming your way.

☆ **Horseshoe:** Tomorrow will be your lucky day!

The tea leaves may give you just one answer to your question or a few. It's up to you and your buds to unravel what the pictures are telling you.

When you look for picture-shapes in the tea-leaves, concentrate on:

☺☺ The shapes that are really clear and easy to spot.

☺☺ The sides of the cup, not the bottom.

☺☺ Tea-leaf pictures near the handle — they're about you.

☺☺ Tea-leaf pictures opposite the handle — they're about buddies and family.

☺☺ Pictures close to the top — they show an event will happen very soon.

So, are you a believer in tea-leaf power? Or girl power? Can the leaves really predict the next day in your life, or is your destiny down to the girl you are and want to be?

What's your   favorite?

Here's a chance for you and your buds to choose some of your favorite things. Get ready to have lots of fun — and to be surprised at what you discover!

What's your hot color?

Do your eyes always zoom in on the same one or two colors? For example, is it ALWAYS pink and purple, and NEVER red and orange? Could it be that colors are tuned into people's personalities? Check out your favorite colors and see. When your buddies take the quiz, make sure they pick out their fave colors before they read the meaning.

Time for change
Your favorite colors and other favorite things can change over time. That's a good thing—it shows you are learning and growing as a person.

Color codes

- **Blue** You prize honesty above all. It upsets you when people pretend to be someone they're not.
- **Green** You're into nature and taking care of people and animals.
- **Yellow** You're always upbeat! Buds like to be close to you in hopes of catching some happiness.
- **Orange** You never miss an opportunity to try new experiences!
- **Red** You have deep passion and commitment. Whatever your cause, you are dedicated to it.

- **Purple** You're a natural leader — fair, trusted, and decisive. You share ideas without seeming bossy.
- **Pink** You're a truly sweet girlie girl. You respect yourself and your buds.
- **Brown** You're a fabulous fun seeker and full of surprises.
- **Black** You're a patient problem-solver who loves to understand more about people.
- **White** You think deeply about big issues, and your buds come to you for advice.

My Favorites Quiz

Pick your favorite color, animal, book, and place to be. Then, choose three words that describe why those things are extra special to you. There are a lot of words to remember, so it's easiest if you write down your answers. To make sure your answers are true to you and only you, try to pick your favorites without talking about them with your friends first. Don't read ahead!

Question 1
What's your favorite color? Choose three words that describe it.

Question 2
If you could be an animal, which would it be? Describe it, using three words.

Question 3
What is your favorite kind of story and why? Pick three words that describe it.

Question 4
Where do you feel totally happy and why? Choose three words that say it all.

Next, copy down these sentences and put your words in the blank spaces. Your color words go into the first sentence, animal words into the second, and so on.

🌸 I am _____, _____, _____.

🌸 My pals like me because I am _____, _____, _____.

🌸 I like to do things that are _____, _____, _____.

🌸 I want my life to be_____, _____,

_____.

How did you do?

Did your feelings about your favorite things measure up? Did they seem to fit perfectly into the answer spaces so the sentences were true? If a couple of your answers don't feel right, it's not a big deal! Maybe you just chose a wrong word or weren't really expressing your true feelings. If this has happened, try again.

Keep a note

When you're happy with your word choices, record them on page 16 of the Grrrl to Grrrl book. Remember to go back and check them in a few months' time.

Soul Secrets sleepover

Looie, Rella, Roxy, and Tutti are always looking
for reasons to have a sleepover! It could be
a birthday, the anniversary of when
they all met, the start of the vacation,
or any time they just want to hang out!

Girls in pajamas are partyin'

Time for action!

Because they are the sleepover supremos, the Grrrls' Girls
have dreamed up enough Soul Secrets games to keep them
laughing from sunset to sunrise. They always learn
something new about one another. So, call your crew
and get ready for action! Rella, Looie, Roxy, and Tutti
want to share their all-time favorite games with you.

The Circle of Life game

Are you confused about something that's going on in your
life? Well, the Circle of Life game will fill you in on what's
happening and how to deal with it. To start playing, find the
Circle of Life game board in your kit. You'll also need a die, the
Numbers Up code on the opposite page, and your best buds!

❀ Each girl takes a turn throwing
the die onto the Circle of Life
board. The circle is divided into
eight categories that relate to
different parts of your life – like
friends, school, and family.
❀ Each number on the die has a
special meaning. You'll find the

meanings in the Numbers Up code.
When the die lands in a section,
look at the number that's facing
up and try to figure out what it
could mean. You might have to
think a bit about how the number
on the dice relates to the Circle of
Life category.

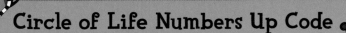

Circle of Life Numbers Up Code

- **1.** All your plans are going to work out. Go, girl!
- **2.** You can rely on your friends to help.
- **3.** Something amazing is going to surprise you.
- **4.** Believe in yourself, and you can make your dreams come true.
- **5.** Take it easy, you're worrying too much.
- **6.** Keep up the good work.

If a die lands on a line or doesn't land on the board, throw the die again.

Dreams for the Future

My Friends

My Hobbies

School Stuff

Circle of Life

Who I Am

My Love Life

Home and Family

Vacation

You also need:
a die, the Numbers Up Code (see page 42 of the *Soul Secrets* book), and your best buds!

If a die lands on a line or doesn't land on the board, throw the die again.

The game ends when everyone has had three turns.

Who do you turn to?

How did you and your friends do? Did the game help you think about what's happening in your life? If you ever need advice on how things are going, where do you turn? Here is a peek. What the Grrrls' Girls do....

I try to find my own solutions.

My Gramma Nellie is so wise. She always helps me.

I read advice columns in magazines, but in the end I make a decision that's right for me.

When I'm unsure about something, I talk it over with Roxy because she knows me inside and out.

Flower favorites

To play the game, you and your buds should each grab a piece of paper. Then write down these five flowers in order, from most favorite to least favorite: Rose, Sunflower, Daisy, Tulip, Daffodil. Once you've got your list, check out the hidden meanings at the bottom of the page. The order you placed the flowers in shows your priorities for the future. The flower you chose as your most favorite reveals what's most important to you. The farther down your list a flower appears, the less important the thing it represents is to you.

Flower Code

Daffodil – Your career plans
Sunflower – Self-esteem and being proud of yourself
Daisy – Family life and caring
Tulip – Money and material things
Rose – Love, friendships, and trust

Makes you think

Did this game help you discover what's most important to you? Was it totally correct or way wrong? The flower game deals with major life stuff, so it's probably given you and your buds lots to talk about. What's most important is that you think about what really matters to you.

Try this

Play the chat room game. It helps you get to know how your buds think. And it might reveal a few things about the way you think, too! You and your friends should sit in a circle. One person says a "starter" word – any word that comes to mind. Then, as you go around the circle, each person says the first word that the starter word makes her think of, like this:
Starter word: "Eskimo"
Rella: "Igloo" Tutti: "Parka" Looie: "Sledding" Roxy: "Ice cream!"
Take turns saying a starter word, and for maximum fun, play the game at mega-speed!

Fishy Fortunes

Take a look in your kit and you'll find a plastic bag.
Inside the bag is the magic fish! Now you're ready to
play Fishy Fortunes.

The magic fish has incredible powers! It can answer any
question you'd like to ask it. You might be burning up to
know if your crush likes you, or if you'll get an A in
geometry. To find out, all you have to do is think really
hard about the question and lay the fish across your
open palm. The fish will then react to your question.
Its body will flap, wiggle, flip over, or curl up!
Watch what the fish does carefully, then check out the
list below to see what message the magic fish has for
you. Keep in mind, you have to ask a question that can
be answered with a "yes" or "no."

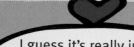 **Magic Messages**

Head flaps about: The waters are murky. Ask again or try another question.
Tail wiggles: Only with a lot of work. It will be an upstream battle.
Flips over: All you have to do is go with the flow.
Sides curl up: Dive right in. You have to act quickly.
Total curl up: There's something bubbling under the surface. Is there something else on your mind?

I guess it's really just a fun game, but when the magic fish predicts something good, then it's fun to believe it!

So, did the magic fish get it right or was it way off target? Roxy's thinking about it ....

And there's more

Listen up! Rella, Tutti, Roxy, and Looie hope you had terrific fun playing the Soul Secrets sleepover games. But if the moon is still up and you aren't sleepy yet, look through this book for the sleepover symbol. Wherever you see it, you'll find more fabulous sleepover fun!

You go, girl!

You and your buds have probably started a billion sentences with phrases like: "When I go to college ..." or "When I have my own apartment." That's because making plans for the future is totally exciting. It's the most natural thing in the world for a girl to do!

The Grrrls' Girls have goals

Rella, Looie, Tutti, and Roxy always think fast forward to the future! Between them, they've come up with thousands of plans for what they want to do and who they want to be. A real Grrrls' Girl listens to her friends' dreams with enthusiasm. She would NEVER put down a bud's ambition — dreams are too special for that!

Every girl has her own dream. Each dream is totally unique, just like you.

I want to be a fabulous fashion designer who creates beautiful clothes that make people feel awesome when they put them on.

I'm not sure exactly what I want to do. I'd love to work with computers or maybe be a doctor. I just want to make a difference. Something as important as my future deserves a whole lotta thought.

My dream is to light up Broadway! (That's where you'll find the best theaters in show biz!) It's not just that I want to be a star – I want to be the most talented actress I can be.

My dream is to be a VJ – a music video jockey! I love music and I know a lot about it. I can just picture myself picking out videos for my show and talking on-camera! It's a perfect job for me.

Dream tips from the Grrrls' Girls

Rella, Looie, Tutti, and Roxy have put their heads together and come up with some ideas to help you keep your plans for the future on track.

Talk to your buds about your plans for the future. It's important to respect your friends' goals – just like you want them to respect yours.

Be true to yourself! Don't worry if your dream is completely different from a lot of other peoples'. Only YOUR dream can make YOU happy.

Listen to your head and your heart! That's where your dreams for tomorrow, next year, and even the next ten years come from!

Remember that lots of dreams take hard work and dedication. Dreams don't always just happen; you sometimes have to work to make them come true.

Write it up

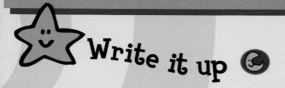

be the girl you wanna be

Ready to talk about your own dreams? You and your buds can write the Dreams for My Future letters inside the kit. When each of you has written down your plans, make sure to sign and date the letters. Fold and seal each one with a "Be the girl you wanna be" sticker. Then, agree on a date – maybe in a year or two – to get together and open the letters. Write down the date you decide on the outside of the letters. When the date arrives, you can open them to see if your dreams have come true, or if you're working hard toward a new, improved dream!

Wild ones follow their dreams until they come true!

YOU GO, GIRL! 47

Be the girl you wanna be!

Rella, Roxy, Looie, and Tutti hope that you and your best buds have discovered a ton of new and amazing things about yourselves, your friendships, and your dreams for the future.

Maybe you're totally tuned into your personality now and are able to understand more about the girl you are.

No matter what you've learned, the important thing is to remember that you are one unique girl with super potential!

When you look in the mirror, see the best parts of you shining through!

As the Grrrls' Girls say:

Believe this deep down, and all the great things in life — best friends, love, fun, and a bright future — will be yours for sure! So, what's next? You just have to keep growing into the girl you wanna be. You have to work to make your dreams come true! And don't forget to keep revisiting and updating your Grrrl to Grrrl book. It's the perfect way to remember everything you and your buds have learned and shared.

Sound off!
Share your thoughts and dreams with the girls of 2 GRRRLS. Keep in touch!

For more **2 GRRRLS** info, and to e-mail us, just look on our site! **www.2grrrls.com**. Here's the address if you want to write:

2 GRRRLS
P.O. Box 75217
St. Paul, MN 55175-0217

See ya later, 'bye!